THE
'POET'S CHOICE'
(Book 1)

by
Henry M. Lyle

COPYRIGHT:

Published by DIROD Publishing
Printed by Amazon UK in Great Britain

ISBN 979-8-4218575-4-9
First Edition

DEDICATION:

This and other books of my poetry are principally dedicated to my dear late wife Annette, who not only shared my love of the Arts, but was my true inspiration. In her absence, I thus commit these to our daughter Connie and to our sons, Richard, Randolph, Raymond and Quentin.

ACKNOWLEDGEMENT:

I am most grateful to Roddy McDowell, who took it upon himself to collate my extensive collection of poetry in such a way that others may enjoy reading them as much as I had writing them.

Without his help and enthusiasm they would undoubtedly have remained gathering dust in some obscure, forgotten folder, never to ever glimpse the light of day.

EPIGRAPH:

Dear Lord accept my gratitude
for guiding me each day,
for being my support through life
and for showing me the way.

Author

BOOKS BY THIS AUTHOR:

SCOTTISH POETRY

NOSTALGIC POETRY

THE POET'S CHOICE (BOOKS 1 - 2)

ONE MAN AND HIS DOGS

POEMS OF FAITH

COUNTRY VERSE

CONTENTS:

REQUIEM FOR BLAIRS:

The cloistered halls are silent now,
the study rooms are bare,
the once proud cradle of the faith
is now no longer there.
The stone and mortar yet withstand
the Aberdeenshire squall
but shelter not the Catholic babes
who heard their Father's call.
*

The chapel which so recently
was lovingly restored
for boys and clergy at the school
to glorify their Lord
will never more resound each day
to carefree boys' acclaim
of what their Lord has meant to them
and why they praise His name.
*

The boys were just like other youths,
although prepared to serve,
the college echoed to their joy,
their lively youthful verve.
For generations Menzies' Hall
has stood there fast
now boys and priestly voices are
just echoes from the past.
*

No longer can receptive minds

be nurtured in the Faith
beneath the clergy's caring wing
kept safe from Satan's swathe.
Now they must strain to hear the call
emitting from the Lord
while battling for their daily bread
among the worldly hoard.

*

Dear Lord I pray, although dispersed
throughout this rugged land
the shepherd of your scattered flock
can bring the lambs to hand.
Somehow, somewhere, some other means
to train the priestly heirs
can yet be found to foster still
vocations bred at Blairs.

THE LETHAL CLOUD:

The deadly pall
creeps slowly o'er the silent land,
both old and young
slumber 'neath its fatal hand.
No warning given,
the killer's stealthy, slow advance
is unannounced
and gives the sleeping souls no chance.

*

Unseen, unheard,
not even a scent to warn the race
who slumber on
in ignorance of the fate they face.
And come the dawn
the hedgerow chorus fills the air,
the sun shines bright,
the world awakes, still unaware.

*

Still unaware
young children skip and dance at play,
without a care
young mothers meet and have their say.
While in their lair
the gremlins of the State conspire
to hide the truth,
the radiation level's higher.

*

They issue lies
to save a tarnished vote or two.
They compromise

the nation's health, to please the few
already rich
on pickings from the nuclear bin
who stand to lose
if moral sense supplanted sin.

*

They're shielded by
the State's obsessive will to hide
all details from
a trusting, lovely world outside
and know full well
a decade on, when victims die,
as Pilot did,
they'll wash their hands and guilt deny.

CHRISTOPHER AND THE OLD MAN:

My heart went out to that small child,
such tenderness displayed,
the thoughtfulness of one so young,
such friendly gestures made.
He gently plucked the simple bloom,
ignored by worldly wise
and stroked the scentless Dandelion,
admired through childhood eyes.

*

'though not the fragrant specimen
we adults much prefer
that child could see a value in
the weeds that flourish there.
Just then an old man chanced to pass,
his aged features drawn,
cold cheerless eyes betrayed his thoughts,
the milk of kindness gone.

*

Just whether Christopher could sense
the old man's heavy heart
or wished with childlike innocence,
a little cheer impart,
he tugged the old man's threadbare coat,
held up the treasured bloom
attempting by that friendly act
to lift the old man's gloom.

*

Alas his ploy for mutual joy
was brushed aside with scorn,
the aged knave so near the grave
repelled the newly born.
The child just smiled and toddled off
to join his friends at play,
I thought how sad that man must be
to treat a child that way.

ISOLATION:

A thousand miles from anywhere,
a thousand fathoms deep,
a thousand souls in concert
as the great cruise liner creeps
across the restless ocean at
the mercy of the waves,
above a world as yet unknown
and hapless seamen's graves.
*

I lean against the rail and feel
the ocean's boundless might
and gaze towards the distant line
where sky and sea unite.
With only white capped waves between
infinity and me
I have a growing reverence for
this angry awesome sea.
*

The wind tears that my flesh and whips
the spray from off the bow
reminding me, we delve as far
as Nature will allow.
How insignificant we are,
how feeble, weak and small
to make these helpless forays mid
this great Atlantic squall.

THE NIGHTMARE:

Young John was not exceptional
in any human way,
just moderately clever and
enjoyed his hours at play;
no more disposed to cruelty
then either you or I
but stamped upon a spider as
the creature ambled by.

*

It hadn't harmed a single soul
as far as Johnny knew
but he just killed the insect, for
that's just what people do
and thoughts of what he'd done to it
completely left his head
until last night he came upon
a spider in his bed.

*

But this time he was minuscule,
the spider was a giant,
with roles reversed John now found that
the spider was the tyrant.
John tried to hide but every time
his sanctuary was breached
no matter where he hid himself
the insect's talons reached.

*

It grabbed the young lad by the leg,
'cause that's what spiders do
and for no reason known to him
it flushed him down the loo.
As John choked in the mighty flush
his mother heard his cries
and woke him from his sleep and he
was back to normal size.

I HAVE NOT GONE:

When I die
I hope my name is carved stone
where I am laid to rest;
remember what I wrote in verse,
at least I did my best
but what lies here's of no account,
in time it will decay,
please look elsewhere for sight of me
since I have passed away.
*
When I die
you only have to leave the hard
dark tarmacadam way
and look among the lush hedgerows
and sapling trees which sway;
right there amongst the greenery
where foxes hunt their prey,
it's there where I would often roam

you'll find my soul at play.
*
When I die
observe men working hunting dogs
in wood or wild hillside,
retrieving game from coverts or
the restless evening tide.
Just watch those gentle labradors
and tell me what you see.

You'll see a dog with game in mouth
and heading back to me.

*

When I die
just listen to the birdsong and
the whisper of the breeze,
the cackle of a pheasant as
he struts among the trees;
the crashing of the cleft waves as
the great ship ploughs on through.
Listen, listen to them all

and I'll be listening too.

*

When I die

please read the many words I've penned,
it may take quite a while

but often it's the goal which makes

the drudgery worthwhile.
You have not buried me in soil,
forgotten for all time,
the most important part of me
will live on through my rhymes.

THE STORM AT SEA:

A thousand miles of ocean to
the nearest solid land,
a thousand reasons we must trust
in God's protective hand;
acknowledging the seamanship
of those with whom we sail
in matters of survival the
Almighty must prevail.

*

No one aboard has any power
to quell the restless sea
or mitigate the angry wind
ignoring prayer and plea.
We're just a speck of humankind
amid this great expanse
and only by the Grace of God
do we stand any chance.

*

The good ship creaks from bow to stern
attacked by pitch and roll,
could we be one addition to
the ocean's tragic toll?
We are so insignificant
within the scheme of things;
is that the mermaid's siren or
the final knell that rings?

*

But once again forgiveness for
the sins that we have borne,
once more we leave the darkness with
no need for kin to mourn.
The great ship's safely cradled us
through Neptune's angry mood
as all who put their trust in her
were confident she would.

THE CHILDREN'S PARTY:

It's party day,
excited children throng the floor;
stampede, akin a mild uproar
with tantalising food galore
and games to play.
*

In groups around,
proud mother's chat, as mothers do
and doleful dads, their presence rue
but each, their little darlings view
with pride profound.
*

They look a treat
in bright bow ties or party dresses,
starched ribbons in the silken tresses;
like little princes and princesses,
all prim and neat.
*

Not anymore,
from carefree frolics in the hall,
the odd mishap, the bump and fall,
the gay abandoned sundry sprawl
upon the floor.
*

Poor mums adopt
this 'such is life' to work undone
all in the name of party fun,
the stains on clothes where ice cream's run
and jelly's dropped.

*

The child once groomed
is so dishevelled and besmeared
and now the aftermath is feared;
for too much food has disappeared
to stay consumed.

THE WAVES AND ME:

Down by the shore, the lonesome shore
beside the restless sea
the restless waves which pound the beach
as so akin to me.
*

At times so gentle as they lap,
they lap the silver sand
and calmly leave the ocean's depths
like Neptune's outstretched hand.
*

My thoughts at times are like the waves,
benign to one and all;
I view the world through kinder eyes
and milder thoughts recall.
*

Another day beside the spray
from angry which pound
and crash with awesome savagery
and terrifying sound.
*

The white spumed rollers meet the land
and deal a vicious blow;
relentless is the ocean's surge,
the mighty tidal flow.
*

Beneath depressing rain filled clouds
marauding breakers charge,
remaining for the time it takes
their flotsam to discharge.
*

Then empty-handed, scurry back
down past the pebbled scree
to reach once more, the murky depths
within the angry sea.
*

Dark moods and pent up energy
are not unknown to me,
once more the similarity
betwixt me and the sea.
*

In days of sheer malevolence

I'm better left alone,

those days of dark self criticism
to which I'm sorely prone.
*

Thoughts wrapped in crass belligerence
when everyone's a foe;
a surface smile belies the fact
I'm smouldering below.
*

So chargers of the ocean's troop
we share a common trait,
we calmly stroke a troubled world
or angrily berate.

THE ANCIENT MARINER:

Brave were the men
who left the safety of the shore
to brave the angry ocean's roar
and knew not when
they'd see both kith and kin once more.
*
They faced sheer hell
in tiny boats, like of which
the murd'rous waves could swamp and pitch,
for what? To swell
the coffers of the land based rich.
*
For umpteen years,
the spouse and father figure gone
his wife and children stood alone.
Through trial and tears
they each in hardship struggled on.
*
Meanwhile 'Jack Tar'
against scurvy, shark and salted meat
and other scourges of the fleet
was sent afar
and knew not when 'twould be complete.
*
He had no say.
At mercy of the chandler's trade
at foreign ports his stops were made
until the day
a cargo bound for home was paid.
*

Then oh what joy,
unsung, approached his cottage door
to greet the child unseen before.
A handsome boy,
unborn when last he left this shore.

LIFE ON A NEED TO KNOW BASIS:

Some natural phenomena
are thrilling to behold
but I am disappointed to
be spoil-sportingly told
the scientific reason for
spectacular displays,
I much preferred the mystery
of less enlightened days.

*

I have no need to know about
the earth's magnetic field,
electrical discharges and
what solar hot spots yield;
how planets tilt and circle in
a never ending dance.
I don't believe in certainties,
believing more in chance.

*

I am thrilled to greet the sun and love
the moon's romantic glow.
Aurora Borealis is
a marvellous night show,
a thunderclap is awesome and
a rainbow is a joy:
I need no exclamation now
nor did so as a boy.

*

A question answered merely meets
a further question, why?
In truth, beyond each problem solved
more ponderables lie.
The need to know distracts me from
the pleasure to be gained
from taking life just as it comes,
unfathomed and untrained.

THE ARCTIC CONVOYS:

A violent death can never be
a less than gruesome end
and just the possibility
most certainly must send
those facing it into a sweat,
a gnawing state of fear
to know an executioner
is ever lurking near.

*

And nowhere must that fear have pained
than in the Arctic Seas
when German U-boats tried to bring
Great Britain to her knees.
They skulked beneath the angry waves
in predatory pose
and all poor souls, their guile un-shipped
immediately froze.

*

Imagine how precarious
a sailor's life could be,
his craft severely tested by
a violent raging sea
and knowing that a U-boat pack
planning annihilation,
unseen, could well be on the verge
of his extermination.

*

But facing danger on all sides
the convoys battled on,
with utmost courage they won through
though many friends had gone.
A starving, threatened Nation owed
those men a mammoth debt.
At peace, the least we now can do
is never to forget.

BAREFACED CHEEK:

The starlet wished exposure at
the movie premiere
and found the perfect answer in
a flash of derriere.
*

While all the bulbs were flashing, with
a touch of barefaced cheek
decided to give everyone
a titillating peek.
*

Manoeuvring to make sure that
the cameras were near
she raised the hemline of her skirt
exhibiting her rear.
*

And to the unconcealed delight
of every husband there
revealed to all the voyeurs that
her sit upon was bare.
*

Her tactic was successful, in
that photos were obtained
and published in the papers, thus
exposure was attained.

RESTRAINT:

Forbidden was hidden a long time ago
and only the good put on view;
now sinning is winning approval and praise
with morals the way of the few.

*

Some say that's the way, be open and gay
with nothing swept under the rug;

let's all have a ball no matter the cost,
restraint is the mark of a mug.

*

But haunted not flaunted was better by far
with discipline ruling the day;
abhorrent's a torrent in no time at all
when stigmas are taken away.

ONE MAN AND HIS DOG:

I love the close affinity
of master with his dog,
unspoken hours in company,
those happy jaunts that jog
the master from lethargic rest,
recumbent in his home
to join his ever doting friend
in wilderness to roam.

*

To man, his dog is simply an
extension of himself,
it's not a pet appendage and
means more to him than wealth.
An incarnation of his moods,
a clone of all he is,
without an independent life
but merely shadows his.

*

Relationships don't come more close
than that of dog to man,
uniquely, never torn apart,
there's nought exists that can.
Based solely on a need to share
the other's company

there's not a partnership on Earth
cemented in this way.

*

Forever loyal, it matters not
his master social class,
a dogs not influenced by wealth
or shuns the lack of brass.
His master's stature in the eyes
of others of his race
means nothing to him, just as long
as he can keep his place.

*

His place is there at master side
and nothing matters more,
through good and bad times they're a team
that's solid to the core.
The lack of dialogue means nought,
it's love that is the tether,
the world at large does not exist
as long as they're together.

*

Age and decay's of no account,
in fact it seals the bond,
with measured hours that lie ahead
a new rapport has dawned.
The years of mellow restfulness,
activity in wane,
a life of sharing, only death
can come between the twain.

TRIPS ASHORE:

We disembark from luxury,
a life of pampered ease;
to stroll amongst a people who
are desperate to please.
*

They scrape a meagre living from
subservience and toil,
in service to the privileged
or labour on the soil.
*

The older generation's lived
through conflict and disease,
experienced oppressive rule
to various degrees.
*

The children grow in poverty
with eagerness to learn
but play and education are
both sacrificed to earn.
*

To earn an utter pittance from
demeaning servitude;
they smile while at the beck and call
of people often rude.
*

We treat those scenes of poverty
as something to admire,
record them with the camera
as objects of desire.
*

What little thought we really give
to hardships tholed by others,
those born of alien cultures are
not always seen as brothers.
*

We rape their hospitality
and see it as our due
and ogle at their lifestyles just
as panoplies to view.
*

Then, with curiosity sufficed,
we retreat aboard our ship
just seeing their existence as
a reason for a trip.

NO HIDING PLACE:

Young people's understanding of
what life is all about
is formed by looking at a screen
ten inches from their snout;
they rarely lift their eyes to see
reality and truth,
the digital distortion is
the preference of our youth.

*

Their life is an addiction to
the 'ping' of contact made
with constant reassurance when
the pointless call is played.
The reassurance that they're still
a member of the gang,
their habit satisfied again
the moment that it rang.

*

The most alarming aspect is
the age at which they start,
provided with a telephone
described as simply 'smart'.
They seem compelled to bare their souls
in such a public way
and then regret the outcome when
cruel bloggers have their say.

*

Their access to a lawless world
that's free from all restraint
exposes them to shameless acts
of every human taint.
Unable or unwilling to
reject life's darker side
technology lays claim to them
with nowhere left to hide.

LEST WE FORGET:

In place of honour, etched in gold
a mighty archway to the bold
stands proudly 'mid the city rush
where each November falls a hush
while low and high born pay respect,
their honest, solemn frowns reflect
a deep and lasting sign of grief
for those whose lives were cruelly brief.

*

But carved on stones not half so grand
in every village in the land
stand poignant mem'ries of a war.
Some crosses honour ten or more
while simple tablets bear just one,

but still one grieving mother's son.

*

Bedecked with poppies once a year
reminders of our loved ones dear,
a focal point for homage shown
for those whose graves are still unknown.
Concise inscriptions proudly tell
their names, their ranks and where they fell,
beneath assurance, so were told.
unlike ourselves, they'll not grow old.
Removed so early from life's stage,
denied the chance to live and age,
I wish our tombstones honoured men
who'd reached three score years and ten.

THE NEW PUPPY:

What have I done?
An eight week untamed Labrador
with claws and sharp teeth to the fore,
a twenty-four hour canine chore
but bags of fun.
*

No rest for me,
it's piles and puddles on the floor
and wiping up for evermore
'til Nell has grasped it's out the door
to have a wee.
*

For weeks to come,
no long lies for a sleepy head
or slipping off for an early bed,

it's constant vigilance instead

o'er my wee chum.
*

Relaxing walks
with well-trained dogs around my feet
admired by everyone I meet
will be a fast forgotten treat
replaced by shocks.
*

As mighty mouse
explores each muddy nook and cranny
and gnaws on anything that's handy;
she's anything but quiet and canny
about the house.
*

But when she lies
asleep or nibbles at my ear,
all thoughts of murder disappear,
I'm happy just to have her near
despite the ties.

*

She's small and weak
and looks to me for everything,
I see in her the hope of spring,
the dog, maturity will bring,
that's all I seek.

MAN AND HIS ALLOTMENT:

Some men appreciate their flowers,
take pride in perfect blooms
and lucky wives appreciate
displays in all the rooms,
but country men find vegetables
an even greater treat,
they find fulfilment growing plants

that they and their's can eat.

*

Allotmenteer or kitchen plot,
he treats them both the same,
a cornucopia of veg
of quality his aim.
He knows the secret's in the soil
and labours to that end,
down close and dirty he thinks of
his compost as a friend.

*

He feeds his soil with fervour on
what ever comes to hand,
manure and compost help improve
the texture of his land
and as the plants show sturdy growth
he diligently weeds,
he nets and waters as required
to meet their varied needs.

*

The fruits of his endeavours come
ten fold at harvest time
with healthy crops to harvest and
consume while in their prime.
A smudge or two, a crooked shape,
a nibble here and there
it's truly little price to pay
for unpolluted fare.

THY WILL BE DONE:

A Son stands in Gethsemane
one faith defining night
where others in such danger would
have surely taken flight;
He knows a dreadful death awaits,
a death nailed to the cross
but peaceful resignation is
His mood that comes across.

*

His friends lie sleeping by his feet,
not one to share the strain
he looks up to his Father to
absolve Him from the pain;
'Father, if it is possible
divert what is to come

but I accept it's not My will
but Thy will must be done'.

*

Outwith the city wall at night
is not the safest place
when one has ruffled feathers of
a touchy Jewish race
and from the shadow of the trees
a brigand band appears
and Jesus knows they've come for Him
and crucifixion nears.

*

His followers awake and say
He preaches all alone,
denying that they see Him as
a King without a throne.
'Which one of you is Jesus,' asks
the Roman with a hiss
and Judas sells his Master with
the traitor's fateful kiss.

OUTSIDE THE PUB:

The mercury is rising and
the lassies' hemlines too,
the young men take advantage, while
the old men simply view.
At eighty-two the temperature
is getting hard to bear;
at eighty-two the old men are
just happy to be there.
*

Girls sizzle 'neath the canopies
and draw the young men near,
the old men are excluded and
they settle for their beer.
The young are hot and bothered but
they never seem to tire,
they build a mighty head of steam,
the old men just perspire.
*

While those just on the threshold flirt
beneath the mid-day sun
the octogenarians talk
of how the War was won.
The youngsters vying for a mate
overtly mix and match;
the old men past their vying days
are happy just to watch.

WHO IS THE ONE?

Who is the one
I know will never let me down,
will have a smile to meet my frown,
will never think of me a clown
or butt of fun?
*

Who is the one
to right the wrongs and calm my fears,
to tenderly erase my tears,
to hold my hand when danger nears
or pain's begun?
*

Who is the one
who drives me on when doubts arise,
who always heeds my pleading cries,
who has those reassuring eyes

that say we've won?
*

Who is the one
I know will still be by my side
when lesser friends desert and hide,
the one in whom I can confide
what I have done?
*

Who is the one
who always greets me with a smile,
is prepared to go that extra mile,
devoid of selfishness and guile
when others shun?
*

Who is the one
who is the fulcrum of my life,
the soothing balm for every strife?
None other than my dearest wife,
she is the one.

MY LOVE AFFAIR WITH PAPER:

Protect me from invasive screens
that multiply unchecked
while I embrace the pen and pad
that most folks now neglect.
I love the comfort of a book
which I can fondly hold,
expansive newspapers which I
caress and neatly fold.

*

The stately homes with libraries
of finest ancient tomes
or book-shelves bearing trivia
in much more modest homes
both captivate and thrill me like
no heartless screen can do,
I love to gently turn a page
not simply click and view.

*

A simple piece of paper is
a gift which warms my heart
inviting words of wisdom and
I cannot wait to start.
It may not be a masterpiece
but who is there to say

that given time it won't take on
significance some day.

*

A simple piece of paper which
is yellowing with age
can be a piece of history
inscribed within a page.
Handwriting, signatures and seals
that freeze a point in time,
to swap that for technology
will prove to be a crime.

WITH MY LORD BESIDE ME:

What is to fear in life when I
have You to walk beside me?
My rod and staff when enemies
in malice, come to chide me;
gain comfort from Your presence when
some wicked tongues deride me.
and with Your strength I can resist
when evil men misguide me.
I'm privileged indeed to have
the cloak of Faith astride me
but if I treat it as my due
then truly woe betide me.

OUR LADY OF THE SEA:

A lifetime spanning many years
or tragically few
as well as love and happy days
brings fear and heartbreak too.
As children, when the knocks of life
brought on a bitter tear
the solace of a mother's arms
was comfortingly near.

*

But age and independence gained
to sail uncharted seas
away from mother's sheltered cove
would generate unease
had we to face life storms alone,
denied a soothing word,
but no, a mother still is near,
the Mother of our Lord.

*

Our Lady never leaves our side
through tempest, toil and tear,
Her gentle presence calms the mind
and quells the waves of fear,
and when life's voyage ends at death
Her help will still be given,
She'll lead us to the safety of
an anchorage in Heaven.

THE HEADLINERS:

The boys and girls of P & O,
who sing and dance with zest,
perform to such a standard as
to rank among the best.
Young men athletic to the core
with skills beyond reproach,
young woman lithe and supple with
a seductive like approach.

*

With songs and rhythm from an age
of innocent romance,
when courtship flourished healthily
in melody and dance.
The leading roles accomplished with
enthusiastic ease,
the dancing girls in 'Tiller style'
with energetic knees.

*

Their repertoire may well have grown
out of an earlier age
but they ensure variety
endures to grace the stage.
Some genres come and genres go
with youthful love of change,
but what the Headliners provide
lies neatly in my range.

NEW YEAR'S RESOLUTION:

The first day of another year,
will this one foster smile or tear
in safe environment or fear?
Just time will tell.

*

With hopes and aspirations high,
no known pitfalls to cloud our sky
we pray that no disasters lie
in wait for us.

*

With fortitude and strength of will
we're set to conquer this year's hill
and think of others good, not ill
just as we should.

*

At twelve o'clock we turned a page,
a chance once more to come of age
discarding all the old year's rage
and selfish ways.

*

A virgin path on which to walk,
a tongue clear of malicious talk,
ambition free of covert stalk
or jealous thought.

*

A will to keep our resolution,
a life unstained by self pollution
in time will prove the right solution
to all life's ills.

ON TO THE HOLY LAND:

Call it a pilgrimage of sorts,
a journey long time planned
but I have always wished to set
foot on the Holy Land.
*

To walk where Jesus trod this earth
to satisfy God's plan,
to sacrifice His precious blood
to save the soul of man.
*

To scan the Sea of Galilee
where fishermen were called
and stand were stood the stable where
the infant Christ was stalled.
*

To tread the dust where He once trod
to spread the Word of God
and hope to hear the call myself
and think that nothing odd.
*

My only wish, to set aside
commercial degradation;
experiencing truer vibes
and undeserved Salvation.

AQUA VITAE:

As Scottish as the heather and
the tartan and the glens,
is synonymous with Auld Lang Syne
and cultivating friends;
as pure as Scotia's highland air,
as clear as a mountain streams
the amber nectar in a glass,
the stuff of Scottish dreams.

*

These days when all we eat and drink
is chemically preserved,
consuming all that poison leaves
me totally unnerved;
whereas, a dram of whisky is
an honest wholesome thing,
just barley, yeast and water from
a crystal highland spring.

MERMAIDS:

Sweet song seductive siren from
your lair beneath the sea
but sensible the sailors who
reject your call and flee.
*

Many are the mariners
lured cruelly to their graves
who sailed towards the lilting airs
that drifted o'er the waves.
*

So innocent and welcoming
you comb your flaxen hair
and gaze into your looking glass,
half fish, half maiden fair.
*

A temptress who has fed upon
the lonely boatman's yen;
indeed, not just poor sailors but
the weakness of all men
*

who wish to be seduced by she
whom other men admire,
to fill the treasured role to which
all others must aspire.
*

A golden goddess, scales alight
which simmer in the sun,
a lure the feeble minded seem
too desperate to shun.
*

Last seen in solemn search for you,
ignoring pleas to turn,
abandoning all common sense
and never to return.

THE DANCING GIRLS:

Parisian follies with full feathered dollies,
fantasies fanning desire;
if dancing girls dress becomes less even less
old men will surely expire.
*
How lusciously lithe and charmingly blithe
they master their sumptuous routine
with synchronised ease as light as a breeze
these girls are deliciously lean.
*
Erotically neat from their head to their feet
in costumes just virtually there;
unless they are near old eyes not quite clear
are tricked into thinking them bare.
*
Such rhythmic exposure shall surely bring closure

on any man's thoughts to retire

from seeking a measure of physical pleasure
with girls in seductive attire.

FICKLENESS:

A female's fickle to extreme
with what may, or may not, be seen;
while bathing in the sun's warm rays
well nigh her total charm displays,
a tiny part of her concealed,
all else quite flagrantly revealed.
*

Now take the sun from the equation,
observe her on a dull occasion;
the puff of wind that lifts her dress
propels her into prim distress,
she struggles with the prying breeze
to keep from view her dimpled knees.
*

Deft fingers to her hemline rush
perchance the show will make her blush.
How farcical, she is perplexed,
what will the wind make public next?
The question now, will fore or aft
be made a feature by the draft?
*

I vouch a damsel in distress
will grip the frontal of her dress
and let whatever may appear
be viewed discreetly from the rear.
Content that combat with the air
is safely won, apart from there,
thus holding fast a modesty
a blink of sun can sweep away.

THE WAVES:

What mighty unseen power controls the waves
and guides them ceaselessly towards the beach
to gouge out rocky headlands into caves
and bring the twisted flotsam into reach?
*
And whipped into a frenzy by the gales,
white-capped they flow triumphant to the shore,
the wind that made them angry, softly wails
while inshore waters marble all the more.
*
The ebb tide leaves the rocks just peeping through
to churn the beach-bound waves into a foam,
they swirl and spray round stones of every hue,
a sweet embrace and promise not to roam.
*
The grimness of the grey relentless swell
is like the sombre heavy clouds on high,
the line 'tween each is difficult to tell,
the blur between the angry sea and sky.
*
The sea birds wheel above the breaking waves
so aerobatic as they ride the rise,
beside the cliffs their artistry them save
from death, mid turbulence within the skies.
*
The wind has dropped, they gently lap the sand,
like tender kisses laid upon the shore,
to ripple up the shallow sloping land
and trickle to the murky depths once more.

SONG OF THE BARLEY:

When balmy summer breezes blow
to cool the blistering heat of June
I hear them whisper soft and low,
it's sad the blade will reach them soon.
*

I hear them rustle in the breeze,
they sadly shake their heads and sigh,
and hold my interest with ease
with looks demure and profile shy.
*

The chatter of the reaper blade,
the clatter of the harvest binder,
no more this year, they'll serenade,
not just to them should fate be kinder.
*

In full submission to their fate
they bow their heads and gently cry,
they cannot flee the reaper's hate,
in truth someday, like them, we'll die.
*

But first it is my dearest wish
once more to hear the barley pray,
once more to hear that gentle swish
as countless golden seed heads sway.

A GLORY MARGINALISED:

Midsummer fields are not the same
without the poppies in the grain,
great seas of green just tinged with gold,
such sterile vistas to behold
where once the popular reigned supreme
and brought to life a sombre scene.
*

Great swathes of crimson in the fields
did nought to lessen farmers' yields
but to responsive passers-by
they were a tonic to the eye.
No other flower can add so much,
towards Nature's true artistic touch.

*

For centuries man has plied his trade
and from the land, a living made;
a living co-existing with
the plants and beasts he shared there with
but armed with chemicals, destroyed
and made the fields a sorry void.

*

Ironic'lly the crimson flower
emblem of man's unselfish hour
when millions suffered death and pain
has been itself, in millions slain.
Now we today must be content
with remnants of a great event.
*

Midsummer's show of scarlet glory
is now a very sombre story;
just here and there, along the path
where they escaped the sprayer's wrath.
Synonymous with loss and tear
the corn poppies of yesteryear.

THE BEACHCOMBER:

Each tide replenishes his trove,
brings hope of treasures new
relinquished by retreating waves,
exposed to human view.
Amid pollutants, debris of
a shameful, wasteful world,
the chance to stumble on a prize
the ebbing tide's unfurled.

*

A hope each day for items from
the wider world out there;
exciting things delivered from
quite simply God knows where.
Did violence seas reach out and snatch
some cargo from a deck
or has the tragic flotsam spilled
from some disastrous wreck?

*

Or merely some unwanted gem
discarded on the seas
and pushed a thousand miles or more
by tidal waves and breeze.
Of little value at its source,
a novelty for sure;
a journey of such magnitude
is cause for its allure.

*

But as a practical pursuit
the beachcomber's no fool,
he gathers sea washed coal and wood
to supplement his fuel.
But Neptune's sculptures are by far
the ultimate reward,
wood carved by motion in the seas
and worthy of award.

THE ENSIGN:

Great Britain may no longer be
the ruler of the waves,
no longer be the naval force
we patriots would crave,
no longer self-sufficient in
the tonnage that we build
nor number one in fire power, the
position we once filled.
*
But, have no fear traditions formed
when we were at our peak
live on in British naval life,
we are by no means weak;
the discipline and excellence
of those who go to sea
still merits well deserved respect
whereever they may be.
*
The Ensign, whether red or white
displayed in any port
on battleship or cruise liner
in holiday resort,
has earned a reputation that
the personnel on board
are of the highest calibre
with seamanship assured.

THE OLIVE TREE:

The Olive tree,
the tree that neither weeps nor dies

yet heard the Holy Women's cries
and saw the Carpenter arise
for you and me.

*

Within its shade
the Son of God would often preach
and through the Parables would teach
the Galilean folks to reach
the home God made.

*

A symbol of
renaissance to a state of peace,

the olive branch is man's release

from sad and intolerances and crease,
back into love.

*

Said by Saint Luke,
it witnessed Christ's ignoble death,
bore witness to his final breath
and saw him rise to Heaven;
sayeth the Holy Book.

ARMAGGEDON:

This planet was a lovely place
a century ago
when humans thrived because the men
could plough the earth and mow;
its downfall started on the day
we harnessed engine power
and stumbled on the chemicals
that turned the sweet earth sour.
*
Unfortunately it is true
we cannot dis-invent
therefore the world is doomed although
we honestly repent.
The planet's only hope lies in
a huge catastrophe,
immeasurably dark to sweep
the whole damn lot away.

THE OLD MAN AND HIS DOG:

Age has stooped the noble frame
and stiffened up the stride,
each unsteady and unsure
but happy side by side.
A shared ambivalence to life,
its quality through pain
but no such doubts, just pleasure in
the bond between the twain.

*

Their walk is just a shadow of
the miles they undertook
when dog brought back the errant sheep
and master held the crook.
They've earned their freedom from the need
to scrape an honest crust,
but years of shared endeavour has
now blossomed into trust.

*

His clothes have seen a better day,
her coat has lost its sheen,
they sit and watch the world go by
and doze off in between.
Few words are passed, but if you watch
a pat or wrinkled smile
says, 'thank you lass for all we've shared
and every happy mile'.

A REAL CHILDHOOD:

The second world wide war was o'er
when I began to play
the simple childhood pastimes I
remember to this day;
the freedom of an open door,
a riverbank near hand,
a cobbled street and honest pals
with very little planned.

*

I ran from early morn till dusk
in energetic games
with bat and ball or nought at all,
just figments of my brains;
imagining what e'er I wished
to emulate that day
and by the use of simple props
turned ideas into play.

*

A bicycle, my passport to
a wider field of joy;
to playing field or swimming pool
or other healthy ploy.
My home was a secure retreat
on stormy winter days,
a mother who was motherly
in all domestic ways.

*

The fireside was a haven in
a sometimes draughty home,
the pattern rug a landscape where
toy animals would roam;
a cardboard box was anything
my fantasy required
and bed was always welcome by
a child completely tired.

*

The wireless met my needs as far
as music was concerned
and storybooks of every sort
the source of what I learned.
Embracing nature as I did,
I cherished all things wild;
compare that simple innocence
against the modern child.

THE SUNSHINE IN MY LIFE:

You are the sunshine in my life,
the subject of my dreams;
whenever I am with you, oh
how precious this life seems.
*

My joy's complete when e'er we meet,
my happiness is won;
without you clouds come rolling in
to disengage the sun.
*

You are the light that guides my way
through dark and gloomy days,
I bask within the soothing warmth
of your unselfish ways.
*

Protecting me from otherwise
self-deprecating traits;
in you lies my salvation from
a dark depressive fate.
*

Warm comfort in a chilly world,
pink glow when all is blue;
when times are hard or lonely,
I need only turn to you.

THE CARDBOARD BOX:

Don't fail to praise
imaginative childhood skills,
those happy hours and sundry thrills
with laughter fun and frolic spills
in play filled days
unburdened by our worldly ills.

*

Unfettered joy,
a cardboard box and youth combined
and freedom of an open mind
create a world to which we're blind
but to a boy,
a box is that for which he's pined.

*

It can become
a spaceship, tank or railway train,
the cockpit of an aeroplane,
the body of a comrade slain,
what endless fun
from what to us would seem mundane.

*

A young girl too
can use a box to great effect,
a pram, her dollies to protect,
a coach and matching pair bedecked
in brilliant hue,
all made from that which we reject.

*

To us, 'though wise,
that box remains an empty shell
and what it was held, who can tell?
But we wise adults know full well
'twill not give rise
to dreams that weave a magic spell.

EXTINCTION:

Humanity should be ashamed
of all the harm we've done,
the plant and creature species that
we've slaughtered one by one.
Where ever we have interests
at odds with Nature's plan
the wildlife needs come second to
the callous whims of man.
*

Superior intelligence
has never been in doubt
and scientific progress is
now littered all about;
deeds close to damn miraculous
are every day events
quite rightly lauded and admired
with minimal dissent.
*

But sinister self interests
pervade enquiring minds
with flimsy ethical restraints
that follow on behind.
But where there's muck there's money
is the earthly wisdom's view
but where there's money to be made,
there's muck a plenty too.
*

The search for profit now exceeds
compassion in our race ,
defection from morality
is spreading at a pace.
Need look no further than the mess
that plastic's left us in
with chemical pollution of
the world and all within.
*

The green and pleasant land I knew
in boyhood is no more,
when last could I enjoy the sight
of partridges galore,
of songbirds by my morning walk
and minnows in each stream?
No friends, that green and pleasant land
is now all but a dream.

LETTERS:

The priceless information as
how our forebears fared
is from the letters, still extant,
because in them they aired
the details of their daily lives,
their triumphs and their fears
and fortunately thoughtful folks
preserved them through the years.

*

Not only do they furnish us
with news of goings on,
a glimpse into a way of life
that's sadly now long gone,
but we can have within our hands
the output of their pen,
handwriting and the signature
of authors way back then.

*

More formal information was
recorded in a book
in masterful handwriting by
a careful scribe who took
the greatest care to leave us with
a record which is true
and in itself, a masterpiece
that's wonderful to view.

*

What will this generation leave
for those who follow on?
A rubbish bin of cyber trash
our printers tend to spawn
with not a single signature
to verify the truth,
a correspondence jungle that's
ill-mannered and uncouth.

JANUARY ANEW:

The hectic celebrations of
the Christmas season's o'er,
the family get-togethers with
indulgence to the fore
and thoughts of summer sunshine breaks
have yet to take a hold,
incongruous while weather's still
so finger numbing cold.

*

It's January and I for one
enjoy the new year's dawn,
long evenings in the lamp light with
the curtains tightly drawn.
It is the sort of month without
the urgency for change,
the urge for novel purchases
and then to rearrange.

*

It's more a contemplative month,
just taking time to think,
remembering the year just past
and any broken link;
the month when people are subdued,
while busy taking stock,
work governed by the daylight hours
instead of by the clock.

*

The January gales can howl,
the frost can take a bite,
the daylight hours can number few
with long hours of the night,
but I still value what it brings
this first month of the year,
a gentle interlude before
fresh life forms reappear.

JUST AN IMAGE:

Look along, admire this lovely world
in all its verdant green,
the clarity of country air,
the sparkling mountain stream.

*

Take pictures of your favoured place
to capture all its charm,
immortalise in prose and verse
the by-ways and the farm.

*

For not too many years from now
if greed is not o'ercome
those images alone will show
the damage we have done.

*

Amid the carnage of our deeds
a child will turn a page
to learn about the loveliness
of this, a bygone age.

MID WINTER'S BALM:

The frozen winter trees among
where crystal chandeliers are hung
and footsteps crunch on virgin snow
on hibernating beasts below.

*

The slanting rays pervade the trees,
paint countless cameos to please;
pink tinge the bark on every bough
entwined by creepers, slumbering now.

*

Appreciate the smothered sound
such peaceful silence all around.
To arctic winds a debt is owed
for Nature in albino mode.

*

A welcome gentle transformation
befits this time of adoration;
the sweet duet of brown on white,
a sombre harmonising sight.

*

Snow-cover deadens raucous noise
enabling more aesthetic joys;
a world anaesthetised and calm
thank God for winter's icy balm.

THE VILLAGE CHRISTMAS TREE:

A buzz about the village shop
for overlooked supplies,
the bonhomie of gentle folks
with salutary cries.
Each cottage tastefully bedecked
with Nature's evergreens
and snow and icicles to crown
the deep midwinter scene.
*

As darkness falls the homely light
peeps out from leaded panes
to give the snow a warmer glow
in silent country lanes.
With noise serenely muffled by
the blanket on the ground
the church bells and the choristers
provide a blessed sound.
*

Devotion draws the villagers
from simple cosy homes
to head towards the little church
beneath a star lit dome,
all mindful of the reason for
their happy Christmas joy
to celebrate the coming of
a tiny baby boy.

A DIGNIFIED ACCEPTANCE:

The many hours of solitude
I spend with pen in hand,
seeking the inspiration to
complete another strand
of literary brilliance or
a miserable attempt
is worth the while if it avoids
posterity's contempt.

*

I feel accepted that I shall
not live to see the day
that my abundant output will
be thought of either way,
feel covert satisfaction in
the knowledge that my rhymes
may entertain successors in
so very different times.

*

Resigned to anonymity
as long as I shall live,
I'm quietly smug in the belief
my work someday will give
some pleasure to the good folks who
appreciate the past,
who jettison the trivia
and to the rest, hold fast.

*

What greater accolade is there
than after I have a gone
to have my cherished views on life
discussed and then passed on?
Of one thing I am very sure
the years of moral change
have not been in his interests
for Man to rearrange.

MY REFUGE IN THE NIGHT:

The air is still,
stars twinkle in the crystal sky,
the moonlight's gentle on the eye;
in such a scene I wonder why
there's grave ill will?
*

To see the world
asleep and bathed in sombre light,
enjoy the silence of the night
it's inconceivable to fight
or insults hurl.
*

It's peaceful when
the rush and raucousness of day
and all the noise is swept away
to be replaced by sanity
and plain amen.
*

The blissful dark,
a refuge from invasive light
and critical destructive sight
into the blind, forgiving night,
my savings are.
*

Secure and free
from judgement, other than my own,
the chance to think and be alone
away from those who would disown
the likes of me.

CHRISTMAS:

December days are short and cold
but Christmas time draws near;
the feast of gross indulgence,
goodwill and cosy cheer.
*

The messages of friendship in
the cards the postman bring
and promise of a better world
as countless church bells ring.
*

When families assemble at
the banquet of the year
and guiding stars are visible
when frosty nights are clear.
*

All base and fractious thoughts are shed
and love is in the air
and erstwhile scrooges of the world
now feel disposed to share.
*

On Christmas Eve excitement grows,
anticipation swells
to carols of the choristers
and sleighs bedecked with bells.
*

The children are beside themselves
in innocent belief
and parents know their time asleep
will certainly be brief.
*

The stockings hung beside the fire
and Santa's snacks prepared
as parents who make dreams come true
hear children's wishes aired.

*

Wide eyes survey the Christmas tree,
a marvel in itself
as figures from nativity
adorn the mantle shelf.

*

This Christmas miracle's complete
and children's faces glow
when, peeking through the blinds, they see
the gently falling snow.

TRUE LOVE:

True love accepts no boundaries,
is infinite and free;
it thrives in wealth and poverty
and where the eye can't see.
*

It can't be bought, it can't be sold
or bartered for a cause
but as a gift, the gift of love's
completely free from flaws.
*

Age is irrelevant to love
when given or received,
from infancy to infirmity
a bonding is achieved.
*

In love the world's a better place
and others irksome ways
no longer seem incongruous
nor draws a hostile gaze.
*

True love is universal, it
transcends all human blight,
is classless, colourless and guides
our ways from wrong to right.
*

From man to man and child to child
one woman with another ,
spouses, lovers, partners all
can deeply love each other.
*

So many forms of love exist,
the parent for the child,
platonic friendships, courtships too
which drives the lovers wild.
*

Love asks no questions, tells no lies
and analyses nought,
it captivates and liberates,
no recompense is sought.

AN OLD MAN'S GRIEF:

For sixty years they shared and cared,
they faced the world together;
to each the marriage vows had been
a blessing, not a tether;
they'd known each other's every thought,
had strived towards their dream
and in their recent twilight years
had been a solid team.

*

Today he laid his wife to rest,
what will tomorrow hold?
He'll have to face life all alone
heartbroken, felled and old.
Back home again to memories,
sad comfort in his grief
his dearest wish, that time apart
is destined to be brief.

*

Her slippers by her empty chair,
her clothes still in the press,
remembering when making tea
to make a little less.
Her spectacles beside her book,
the bookmark still in place,
their wedding photo on the shelf,
the starched and ironed lace.

*

It's almost though she's just nipped out
to purchase what they lack
but sadly he knows very well
she won't be coming back.
He holds her jersey to his cheek,
her scent still lingers on
how long he wonders wistfully
before it too has gone?

*

So many things he'll have to learn
which she attended to,
so many firsts without her there,
ordeals to struggle through.
Alone at night, he thinks of her
in unrelenting pain;
in tears he nurtures his belief
that they will meet again.

WHEN LIFE WAS ALL TOMORROWS:

I've not completely given up
on sweet anticipation;
the joy in what may lie ahead
and my participation
but evermore my thoughts return
to years of useful zest
and things in each tomorrow which
I wished so much to test.

*

The yesterdays were history
from some old dusty tome,
long past and forgotten, life
was from that moment on.
i looked ahead with confidence
to what could lie in store:
a bird just taken to the wing
and desperate to soar.

*

Round every corner lay in wait
some novel things to do,
no life experience to cloud
my clear as crystal view
of what I deemed my promised land,
a cauldron of excess
where all ambition would be met,
all quests end in success.

*

When roots were anchors binding me
to what had gone before;
to standards I rebelled against
in eagerness for more
and life has largely done just that,
delivered even more
but now I feel nostalgia for
the way things were before.

THE SILVER ANNIVERSARY:

The silver threads of happiness
that stretch into the past
to prove that true devotion can
quite undiminished, last;
what passing years can tarnish, nor
the trials of life impair
are all the little thoughtful things
that loving couples share.

*

Eight thousand days of harmony,
eight thousand days of joy,
eight thousand intimate routines
that those in love employ.
A silver tongue on silver sand
beneath a silver moon
can prove a quarter century
has slipped by all too soon.

*

With closeness ever greater and
a mutual trust secure
the potholes of life's route become
less bumpy and much fewer.
In overt sweet reliance we
are beacons to our peers
that marriage can get stronger with
the passing of the years.

FRIENDSHIP:

True friendship is an abstract term,
intangible, yet real;
its values lie not in a cost
but in the way we feel.

*

With strength to bear a thousand tiffs
and know just when to yield,
it thrives on honesty and trust
where nothing lies concealed.

*

It bridges race, it bridges class,
has colour blindness too
and nought can force itself between
a friendship which is true.

I FEEL NO NEED:

I feel no need of knowledge as
to why a thing is so,
it does not pain me that I am
so seldom in the know.
If I can muddle through without
the answer to all things
then that is what I do and bask
within the peace it brings.

*

I'm not expected to achieve
and never lead the pack,
cut loose from those in front who scorn
the souls behind their back.
They worry, envy and mistrust
all those they deem a threat,
contentment is a state of mind
they've not to this day met.

*

I feel no need of knowledge which
is of no use to me,
amassing information, just
a scholar type to be
strikes me like weighing down one's self
with baggage in excess
of that which clearly contributes
to personal success.

*

Success is pure conjecture, it's
immeasurably vague
and slavishly pursuance is
the universal plague.
The gift of healthy life exceeds
success in every guise,
I have my wife, I have my health
and need no further prize.

LOVE CANNOT FAIL TO WIN:

When all life's inextricable
experiences are weighed
with all reactions analysed
and all conclusions made.
Out shining all, omnipotent,
and selfless reign above
the ordinary traits of life
undoubtedly lies love.

*

Love is the start, the end and all
that matters in between;
it is the kernel of our life
both overt and unseen,
a reason for existence and
survival after death,
as crucial as a heartbeat and
continuous as breath.

*

A fountain of emotions which
erupt unceasingly,
a power for good no selfishness
can morally betray.
Love cannot be eclipsed or hide
beneath a veil of sin;
love in the end will conquer all,
love cannot fail to win.

FIELD SPORTS:

In times of russet mellowness
when autumn takes the stage
the pace of rural life dips as
the year begins to age.
We country folks who toil from dawn
'till sunset every day,
in winter's shorter daylight hours
find time once more to play.

*

The coverts and the open moor
draw men of hunting mind
who use the skill of eager dogs
to see what they can find;
wild-fowlers on the wind swept shore
await the morning light
and by the lakes and rivers stalk
the mallard's evening flight.

*

The fields of golden stubble mean
we've freedom now to roam;
from hides we drop the pigeons on
their evening flight paths home
and those of braver horsemanship
on cold, crisp days are found
in colourful abandonment
in close pursuit of hounds.

*

Participation is the joy
where field sports are concerned,
traditional accomplishments
undoubtedly well earned.
The skills passed down from age to age
are sportingly applied
and damn the vengeful folk who feel
that we should be denied.

THE MOODS OF LOVE:

Love can be a torrid rage
in which we vent our feelings,
a nasty, hurtful war we wage
with wounds so slow in healing,
the more intense the lovers' reign
the more it's loss will lead to pain.

*

Love can be so calm and still
in mutual relaxation,
with neither having urge or will
to break the sweet sensation;
a warm embrace, no word is spoken,
a loving bond which can't be broken.

*

Love is often shrill and bright
with joyful, happy laughter,
two yoked together, sheer delight
to savour long years after;
the gay abandonment of youth,
pursuers, both of joy and truth.
*

Love can be a burning fire,
an all consuming passion
where thoughts of lust and pure desire
erupt in thrilling fashion;
the tiny seed of life transposed,
two lovers lie in sweet repose.
*

Love can be like autumn time,
the bonfire's dying ember,
residual heat from fire of prime,
their urgent youth remember;
now sweet companionship engage,
the mellow bliss that comes with age.

A COCKTAIL OF EMOTIONS:

True love conveys the smitten heart
into the labyrinth
where, blinkered to the wider world
an aphrodisiac plinth
presents the subject of desire
aloft for admiration,
the source of all embracing joy
and godlike delectation.

*

Love is a maze where ordered thoughts
dissolve in disarray,
lucidity does not exist
and selfless actions play.
Euphoria is commonplace,
reality floats by;
it has no place in paradise,
the land where lovers lie.

*

Love is a cocktail of desires
to give and to obtain,
emotions touched by tender words
that pass between the twain.
The pain and passion, joy and woe
that those in love must bear,
that mixture of emotions which
a loving couple share.

THE LADY IN MY LIFE:

As sure as summer follow spring
and swallows come and go;
as sure as rivers greet the sea
and spring tides ebb and flow
there's nought shall drag as twain apart,
the captor of my shackled heart,
the lady in my life.

*

She is the spring time of my dreams
and chases winter chills;
she is the dawning of the day,
relief from nightmare's ills;
she is the balm for things which chide,
life's simply kinder by her side,
the lady in my life.

*

Who else can see my darker self
and love me just the same?
She witnesses my foolishness
then covers up my shame;
superior in every way,
accepts the lesser part to play,
the lady in my life.

*

Who else when wronged and sorely grieved,
or wounded and in pain,
could find it in a generous heart
to hold me yet again?
No one forgives the way she can,
there's known to me no other than
the lady in my life .

*

For these charms and for many more
too numerous to tell
I'll love her and quite willingly
be subject to her spell.
No other has her beauty, charm;
comforts and keeps me safe from harm,
that lady is my wife.

THE SILENCE:

Listen, here the silence,
the silence of the night,
the night without the sense,
the sense of perfect sight,
the sight to see my friends,
my friends whom I hold dear,
hold dear 'till this life ends,
life ends and I can hear,
can hear again the silence,
the silence of the night...

*

HEAVEN:

Heaven is not away up there
or somewhere we can't see;
it's not conditional on what
is done by you and me.
It's where we feel at ease each day,
it's someone whom we love,
it's joy and friendship, smiles and peace
not, out of reach above.

THE FUNERAL:

It was a lovely day to say
'goodbye, we miss you so'
it was a lovely day when we
were forced to let you go.
The sun shone bright, the birds sang out,
all with the world seemed well.
I smiled outwith, but cried within,
could no one really tell?

*

I greeted family and friends
I hadn't seen for years,
exchanging anecdotes of you
while choking back the tears;
dark suits for marriages and deaths
once more pressed into use
by kith and kin from extrovert
to virtual recluse.

*

Your every act was pondered on,
your every tale retold
with universal comfort from
the fact that you were old.
We laughed at things that made you laugh,
regretted your sad blows
but what you thought of each of us
for sure, God only knows.

*

You kept your council to yourself,
withheld the critics tongue;
ignored our bumptious attitude,
the weakness of the young.
You soaked up life's injustices,
your life's demands were few;
oh what I'd give my dearest aunt
for one more day with you.

YOU CAN WIN:

Life is for living and loving anew,
arising from mishaps that happened to you,
don't give in, don't give in.
Life does not always bring things that you like
but it does not end when tragedies strike,
don't give in, don't give in.
*

Downfalls don't mean that you can't rise again,
there's always an outcome from setbacks and pain
raise your chin, raise your chin.
The end of one page means the start of another,
dig deep when you feel you can't go any further,
raise your chin, raise your chin.
*

There's never a hill that hasn't a top,
there's always a base at the foot of a drop,
you can win, you can win.
Dawn always appears at the end of the night,
just pick yourself up and head for the light,
you can win, you know you can win.

HOW DO YOU TELL HIM?

Some things in life are hard to do
and in my time I've had a few
but I can tell you worst by far,
the one that's left an awful scar,
was telling my wee Quentin why
his mummy was about to die.

*

*There is no easy way to tell
a child of just eleven,
within a day or two his mum
will leave and go to Heaven.*

It's bad enough in adult years
to understand the need for tears,
why random tragedies occur,
why cancer took a grip of her,
but aged eleven could he try
to understand why she must die?

*

*There is no easy way to tell
a child of just eleven,
within a day or two his mum
will leave and go to Heaven.*

Shock, pain and sorrow numbed his mind
as reasons why, I failed to find;
the words of comfort can assuage
the grieving at a tender age;
no words, no matter how you try,
explain why his mum has to die.

*

There is no easy way to tell
a child of just eleven,
within a day or two his mum
will leave and go to Heaven.

*

If I am spared a hundred years
I'll not forget those painful tears;
that look that pierced me to the heart
when he was told she'd soon depart.
How could his father just stand by
and let his lovely mummy die?

*

There is no easy way to tell
a child of just eleven,
within a day or two his mum
will leave and go to Heaven.

THE LENTEN LILY:

The Lenten abstinence
is drawing to its welcome close
and winter, when the country froze;
now, nearer the date when Christ arose
from death for man's offence.
*

On Blessed Easter Day
our Lord arose; the sun does too
and paints the world a golden hue.
That gilded scene comes second to
the daffodil's display.
*

A welcome splash of gold
to herald in the springtime cheer,
the resurrection of the year;
a mass of golden trumpets clear
away sad winter's cold.
*

The chill of lent departs.
A sweeter yellow can't be found,
a priceless carpet on the ground.
The Lenten Lily is renowned
for mending broken hearts.

TREASURES OF LOVE:

Seek not the treasure in the earth
or sunk beneath the waves;
the pot of gold at rainbow's end
which we are prone to crave.
Seek love, abiding, honest love
and if you do succeed
then any other mammon quest
is foolishness indeed.

*

If love is yours to have and hold
its value is immense;
you've treasure more than any man,
a blessing more intense.
For love is treasure, have no doubt,
they are one and the same,
and he who has another kind
has treasure just in name.

THE WREATH:

I walked along the riverbank
as I am want to do
and found that someone else had loved
to walk along there too,
a wreath of wild flowers lay beneath
a swaying willow tree,
a scribbled note attached to it
conveyed this heartfelt plea...

*

'This was my Grandpa's favourite spot,
he often came down here;
a kind old man, a country man,
his pleasure was to hear
the birdsong and the rippling stream
and Grandpa used to say
that he could even hear her voice
since Grandma passed away.
*

But recently his visits here
were few and broke his heart
as cancer driven frailty took
that proud old man apart.
Please leave these flowers to mark this spot
my Grandpa died today
and now with Grandma by his side
he won't be far away.'

THE SIMPLE THINGS IN LIFE:

The widely held belief today
that pleasure must be bought;
that prudent ways and poverty
degrades the poor man's lot
is such a sad reflection on
the avarice today
with happiness the product of
ability to pay.

*

The trouble is, our brain controls
emotions of the heart,
we're cleverer than ever but
have lost the simple art
of looking to our blessings, not
good fortune we may crave,
just no amount of worldly wealth's
of use beyond the grave.

*

A joy as simple as fresh air
or health and strength to roam,
sufficient means to do our turn,
a comfortable home;
support of family members in
a show of mutual love,
a bond we feel and know exists
but never need to prove.

*

The joy of peace and quiet to
recall the years gone by,
the happiness and tragedy
that made us laugh or cry;
a conscience free of guilt or gripped
by genuine remorse,
acknowledging tho' times are hard
for others it is worse.

*

To go to bed in comfort, free
from worldly woes and pain,
in equal measure to enjoy
the sunshine and the rain.
The key however to success
regards the simple life
lies in the mutual love and trust
shared with a valued wife.

TWENTY MILES FROM ZERO:

The mushroom burst,
heat seared faces, blistered, scarred,
human torches caught off guard,
mothers cursed
and cried in the silence.
*

The cruel wind,
raped the flesh, laid it waste,
even the young, innocent and chaste
who'd never sinned,
died in the violence.
*

The sinister showers,
no escape, unseen spores,
sickness, withering, malignant sores,
requiem, flowers, superpowers,
a triumph of science…

THE CANDLE OF LIFE;

Lord, may I shed a little light
to breach the darkness of the night,
please shield me from the winds of sin
for I would dearly love to win
against temptations of the deil
and not neglect my sworn ideal
to use my three score years and ten
to serve you Lord on earth, and then
perhaps I'll see you with my eyes
I pray soon after my demise.

THE OLD COMRADE:

The guns are long since silenced and
the bugle calls no more,
most comrades who survived the war are
no longer to the fore;
the body that once charged the foe
is bent and weakened now
but still as independent as
his frailty will allow.
*

His, was the war to end all wars,
the hell of gas and trench
with corpse and rat for company
amid the awful stench;
salute those few old men who are
alive to tell the tale,
the awful horror of Verdun,
the Somme and Passchendaele.
*

For more than eighty years he's lived
with sadness in his mind
for all those brave young innocents
he knew, but left behind.
Throughout a long and varied life
these memories he's kept hold
of how a generation was
deprived of growing old.

THIS LAND:

Land of the purple hill and glen,
home to a warlike race of men
where clansmen rallied to the flame
and gathered in the Prince's name.
*

Land of the Jacobite and plaid,
the broad sword and the cattle raid,
the tartan and the keen skean dhu,
the lonely glen, home of the few.
*

Land of invention, literature,
research, discovery and cure,
of men with letters to their name
from whom both truth and wisdom came.
*

Land of the shepherds on the hill,
the lassies sweating in the mill,
the gillie by the mountain stream,
forerunners in the age of steam.
*

Land of the mighty copper still
and masters of the ink and quill,
tough men who bravely dug for coal
and men who caught the deep sea shoal.
*

Land of the fiery molten steel,
the hardy fishwife bearing creel,
land where the finest ships were made
and shoreline chandlers plied their trade.
*

A land where fearless leaders led
and where traditions were not shed,
a people who were never cowed,
a land of which we're justly proud.

THE ORIANA GRACE:

Dear Lord accept our gratitude
for guiding us each day,
for being our support through life,
for showing us the way.

*

And now as we unite to dine
and see this spread before us
in true humility we join
to thank you Lord in chorus.

*

But may we ask one favour Lord
as this food meets our lips
is there some way that you can stop
it's settling on our hips.

TRAPAIN:

A gentle walk from Haddington
due east along the Tyne
will take you to the mighty knoll
that's stood the test of time.
What ancient glaciers failed to scathe
man now has racked with pain,
he's cut a wound into the heart
of our beloved Traprain.
*

That once proud seat of Lothianers,
raised safe above the foe,
has been incised and crushed to make
the winding roads below.
And early in this century
she yielded priceless gold
left buried 'neath her verdant sod
by legionnaires of old.
*

As long as man has roamed these shores
Traprain has stood on guard,
now sullied by the hand of man
she's like a ragged shard,
and yet when viewed from Haddington
she still can weave a charm,
I pray our much admired Traprain
may come to no more harm.

AN EVENING THOUGHT:

The twilight hour is here,
another day is done,
the fireside brings its cheer,
has God or mammon won?

*

Another day has slipped
away beyond recall
have those in need been helped
in matters great or small?

*

Can you in conscience say
your hand upon your heart
these daylight hours have seen
you play the Christian part?

*

If not, it's not too late,
you cannot change today,
but it will help tomorrow
tonight to kneel and pray.

APPEARANCE IS ALL:

The wife preparing vegetables
who finds to her dismay
some creepy crawly creatures in
an ugly bug display
should feel a rush of pleasure in
the knowledge that this means
a load of noxious chemicals
have not be besmirched her greens.

*

The insects can be washed away
without a risk to health
but damaging insecticides
have more to do with wealth.
Cosmetic aided beauty where
appearance reigns supreme,
a false facade of goodness while
the harm remains unseen.

INNOCENCE AND PLAY:

The halcyon days of childhood half
a century ago
that only people of my age
were privileged to know.
The world sadly has now moved on
discarding on the way
the carefree opportunity
for innocence and play.
*

The junior school where friendships grew
and discipline took root
with exercise encouraged by
arriving there on foot;
a classroom warmed by open fires
and desks set in a row
with teachers treated with respect,
oh for the status quo.
*

Religion and tradition topped
the list of what we learned,
we soon found out success and praise
was only ours when earned.
The history of Scotland was
enshrined in every line
from Bannockburn and Robert Burns

to Queen Victoria's time.

*

Outwith school hours our neighbourhood
was ours to roam at will
with no concerns that anyone
bore children any ill.
We played and thought as children should,
curtailed in what we knew

and learned of life's more sombre side
in stages as we grew.

THE RIVERBANK:

There's magic on the river bank
beneath the willows, cool and dank,
were coots and moor hens, ducks and voles
and scuttling rats from dyke-foot holes
play out their lives as nature will
and once, men toiled within the mill.

*

The mill is quiet, the wheel at rest
as are the folks who gave their best,
but still the stream glides slowly by,
a place of peace for you and I.
A place where time itself stands still
to honour those who worked the mill.

*

Reflections, as the water lies
arrested 'neath the summer skies,
where midges dance and brown trout leap
and herons still as sentries keep.
Where sunlight fractures on the weir
and lush green banks sprawl ever near.

*

The virgin winter, too is grand
when ice and snowflakes bleach the land,
on darkened waters white swans show
and creeping ice restricts the flow.
Where only as the white banks squeeze
do active waters beat the freeze.

*

From mighty rivers two miles wide
to trickles by the meadow side
a flowing stream becalms the mind.
Just close your eyes and you will find
that pressures of the present day
like fallen leaves, just drift away.

PEACE:

Peace, a walk to a distant field
in early morning haze
to fetch the placid milk cows in
from meadows where they laze.
Peace, the solitude I feel
far from the city crowds,
the softness of the morning breeze
dispersing fleecy clouds.

*

Peace is warmth in morning sun
before the world is roused,
the stately pace of milking herds,
those friendly docile cows.
Peace, the dance of countless flies
on iridescent wings,
they spiral in the golden dawn
above all earthbound things.

*

Peace is muffled lowing heard
from muzzles soft and warm,
the shuffling of the cloven hooves
on dusty lanes at morn.
Peace, the song of woodland birds
before the world can hear,
the whirr of crickets in the verge
that stops as I draw near.

*

Peace, the golden shaft of light,
a staircase to the sky
suspending tiny grains of dust
like gems before my eyes.
Peace is scent of dewy grass
still damp from twilight hours
which later dries and fades to leave
the heady scent of flowers.

*

Peace is true companionship
of collie at my heel.
She questions not my every move
nor moods need I conceal.
Peace, the feel of yielding soil
the highways left behind,
just kindly turf on which to walk
with time to clear my mind.

*

Peace I found as dairyman,
I loved that humble chore,
when tending to my gentle beasts,
no man could ask for more.
Peace, this cowman's recompense
for weary hours of toil,
to me such kingly ransom paid
for labour on the soil.

SPRING:

What joy to see the first spring buds
on erstwhile dormant trees,
with promised days beneath the sun,
relief from winter's freeze.
The birds once more begin to nest
and sing from early dawn,
both beast and bird begin to pair
to take the species on.

*

Bare fields as if by magic flush
with grass and meadow flowers
and woodland, skeletal and drab
becoming leafy bowers.
The hum of insect's beating wings,
the call of courting beasts,
the blossoms on the fruiting trees
that promise autumn feasts.

*

The busy chirp of nesting birds,
the drone of working bees,
the heady scent of new mown lawns
where we can take our ease.
Such dormancy to newborn life
now that spring is here
gives hope, when hope it's needed most
to change despair to cheer.

THE BATTLE'S O'ER:

In uniform you paid the price,
you made the final sacrifice
that we may live in peace today.
For that with thanks we humbly pray
the battle's o'er now, peace is won
so rest in peace, our loving son.
*

As we who live, lay you to rest
in peaceful sleep below
in ten life times we'll not repay
the painful debt we owe.
*

Your memory will outlive the war
through freedom which you struggled for
as long as we, love you, tell
the selfless way you fought and fell.
The battle's o'er now peaces is won
so rest in peace, our loving son.
*

As we who live, lay you to rest
in peaceful sleep below
in ten life times we'll not repay
the painful debt we owe.
*

Your picture's proudly on display
and thoughts of you fill every day;
your medals cause a heartfelt tear
and always will, year after year.
The battle's o'er now, peace is won
so rest in peace, our loving son.

As we who live, lay you to rest
in peaceful sleep below
in ten life times we'll not repay
the painful debt we owe.
*

The manner of your death was brave
with glowing words upon your grave
but dearly wish that we could hold
a soldier son not quite so bold.
The battle's o'er now, peace is won
so rest in peace our loving son.
*

As we who live, lay you to rest
in peaceful sleep below
in ten life times we'll not repay
the painful debt we owe.
*

A flag draped coffin, probably borne
by grim faced friends in uniform.
How eerily the last post sounds
as you're laid gently 'neath the ground.
The battle's o'er now, peace is won,
good night, God bless you, loving son.
*

As we who live, lay you to rest
in peaceful sleep below
in ten life times we'll not repay
the painful debt we owe.

STORM DAMAGE:

Chill is the wind that shakes the trees
the winter woods among;
eerie the sounds that greet the ears
the creaking anthem sung;
fleeting the glimpse of bounding deer
protective sinews sprung;
ragged the scene, the aftermath
with storm torn debris hung.

*

Combed by the vicious northern gales
the weak and aged fall;
torn by the force of nature's wrath
receive an early call;
destroyed, dishevelled and unkempt
after the mighty brawl;
sad victims to uneven test
against the tireless squall.

*

Well trodden paths negotiable
with detours here and there
or climbing over fallen boughs
surmountable with care;
the lonely woods are vandalised
with disenchanted air,
a devastated wilderness
which looks beyond repair.

*

But just as Nature can destroy
she can regenerate;
young saplings now can benefit
from others tragic fate.
the brushwood is a sanctuary
where beasts proliferate;
I never fail to marvel at
life's urge to reinstate.

DO YOU REMEMBER?

Do you remember when
as children we went out to play
as long as it was light
and parents taught us right from wrong,
to always be polite,
authority must be obeyed
or punishment ensued
and patience was a virtue when
for most things we just queued.
*

Do you remember when
a debt was unacceptable
and chastity a must,
cohabiting unwed was a sin
and life revolved round trust,
a man's word was reliable
and loyalty was rife
rewarded in all sorts of ways
in many walks of life?
*

Do you remember when
our Britishness was not in doubt,
the question never rose,
we skated on the local pond
in winter when it froze,
when we could leave our doors unlocked
and police were on the beat
and locals were the only folks
whom we could chance to meet?
*

Do you remember when
our farms had poppies in the fields
and chickens running free,
when Christianity held sway
and birds filled every tree,
when young girls' only aim in life
was setting up a home
and young men dreamed of marriage and
a family of their own?
*

Do you remember when
'twas men who wore the trousers and
were deemed the family's head
and women wore nice dresses and
made sure they all were fed,
when neighbours were not strangers and
what mite they had was shared,
they helped each other not for gain
but just because they cared?
*

Do you remember when
the girls had hour glass figures and
young men were usually fit,
when grannies had grey hair and pa's
were stooped but coped with it
and if you do you must have lived
as least as long as me
and doubtless, like me, you preferred
the way things used to be?

**Enjoying this varied and
eclectic series of poetry,
then savour much more in
Book 2**

Printed in Great Britain
by Amazon